CHELSEA'S FOREVER GARDEN

Written by

Laura Lamb

Illustrated by Mary Barrows

For more information, contact the writer at istar63155@bellsouth.net.

ISBN Paperback: 978-1-7375344-0-2
ISBN eBook: 978-1-7375344-1-9

First Edition 2021

Published in the United States of America

Printed in the United States of America

DEDICATION

To the extraordinary souls who guided me to my own forever garden, taught me to honor all life and its rhythms, and opened my eyes to the heaven within.

The old screen door flew open as Chelsea darted out her country home's front door. It was a warm May evening. The bugs were already buzzing and dancing all around her. She rushed to the right and impatiently scanned the yard. She saw nothing out of the ordinary. She retraced her steps and surveyed the left side of the family home. Still, no discovery was made.

Out of breath, Chelsea pleaded to her parents,

"Where?!? Where is it? Is it true? You are giving me my very own plot of land to do with what I please? I can't find it!"

"It's around back of the house on the river side of the barn. Go see! Your mother and I even put a little white fence around your garden. We hope you like it! You've been asking for an area all your own for some time now," declared Daddy.

Chelsea ran to the area of the large,
rural yard her father described.
She could not believe her eyes!
She spotted the most glorious section of
woodlands she had ever seen!
It had always been there, but now this spot
seemed to speak to her.

Chelsea looked beyond the delicate white picket fence. Insects, both crawling and flying, bustled here and there. Flowers strained to peek out above the tall grasses. After opening the gate, she fell to the ground. She hugged this sacred soil that was now her very own. Chelsea could not remember ever feeling so much joy before!

She thought to herself, "What should I do with my small piece of the earth? Should I pull out all the weeds?"
She surveyed her surroundings and noticed the weeds had flowers blooming on them.
Bees were feeding on those flowers.
"Nope," she said out loud.

"Hmmm, should I plant a vegetable garden?" She immediately felt sadness in her heart. Chelsea realized that would ban all the friendly crawling and hopping visitors. Her choice became clear! This space was perfect how it was! There was already so much natural beauty.

Week after week, Chelsea would pop out of
bed in the morning. Her first thought was
how she could spend her free time in her special
garden. She learned some wildlife
appeared in the mornings. They were
not the same as those that came in the
afternoons or evenings. So she learned
to honor the rhythms of her land.

She watched the collective
teamwork of ants. They could carry objects
much larger than themselves. She studied the rabbits.
They could fit between the pickets and would come and
go as they wanted. She played with frogs and
lizards and worms of all shapes and sizes. The winds
made the plants sway and hug tightly to each other
sometimes. Birds particularly loved this garden.
They would bring with them their melodious songs.

Chelsea could lie on her back for hours.
She would watch the puffy, white
clouds drift above her head. She liked to
search for familiar shapes in them. Bottomless
happiness and curious observations filled her days.
In this simple rectangle, the outside world didn't exist.
Nature had become her favorite companion.

There were no prisoners inside Chelsea's garden. She celebrated each arrival. Then guests were bid a loving "Hope to see you back soon" upon their departure. When she was inside this happy place, she felt freedom deep within her. She wanted to gift the same thing to all the life surrounding her.

Other changes began to happen as she spent time in her garden. She was more patient with her younger brother, Anthony. Things used to drive her crazy about him. Now they seemed not a big deal at all. At times, his silly antics would even cause her to giggle.

She found herself whistling and singing throughout the day. It didn't matter if she was in her garden or not. She didn't mind doing her chores or homework either. The whole day seemed brighter. Her heart was fuller, and her smile lasted longer.

The only sad days Chelsea experienced were the days it rained. She would sit by the window and watch the life in her garden. It seemed beaten down by strong rains and sturdy winds. She saw the flower heads droop and wondered if this was how flowers cried. Her new friends would all run for cover as the weather pounded the ground around them. She knew she could not stop the rains from coming. For a moment, this realization caused her sadness. Then she became aware of something quite amazing.

The day after a storm, the plants and animals seemed more alive and energetic. The flowers stood a little taller. Their colors shined a little brighter. The crawling creatures moved from the bottom to the top of the plants. The worms found their way to the surface and the sunlight. The bunnies hopped higher and were more playful with each other. Even the air smelled fresher after a storm had passed through.

Everything seemed washed anew, triggering new growth. Chelsea became aware of another gift from her precious garden. She now knew that both sunshine and storms were needed for the best growth.

Each year, time for school came around. She would see the flowers' blooms turn to seed heads. Squirrels and birds would need those seeds and nuts for the winter months. As colder weather came, many of her bird friends left. She knew they were looking for warmer gardens farther south. In the winter, she noticed how the snow provided a blanket. All her hibernating and burrowing animal companions who remained could stay warm enough. Then the snow would melt, giving way to small sprigs of green breaking through the barren grounds. The animals and insects would once again return to her special garden to teach her. She watched this cycle for several years. She learned to appreciate nature's clock with the changing of the seasons.

As the years mounted, she visited the garden less and less. Her preteen and teenage years called her away for social and academic reasons. Her garden showed signs of Chelsea's neglect. The fence lost some pickets. No more flower heads towered above the soft grasses. Sticker bushes now littered her once sacred space. The birds' songs went mute. The bunnies and their babies abandoned this section of yard. The overgrowth hid the small creatures and insects that once brought joy to her curious eyes.

Other changes outside her garden started to occur. Her brother returned to being bothersome. The weight of her chores and homework felt like a ton of bricks. She wondered what had happened. Her underlying joy and excitement for each day disappeared.

One day in particular as she walked in a city park, Chelsea was feeling extra downhearted. She found herself longing for those carefree days. The ones spent within her white picket fence.

Back then, time was filled with joy.
Gentle breezes tickled her face.
Shadows danced
as the sun moved
across the sky. Oh! And those
cloud-puffed skies where her
imagination often roamed...
Where were they now?

Back then, happiness spread from her head
to her toes. Peace, joy, and freedom had filled
her heart. It all seemed so lost to her now.

In despair, Chelsea plopped herself down. She landed under the cascading boughs of a weeping willow tree. She closed her eyes to the world around her. She let her heart cry out for that childhood scenery. She mentally pictured herself where she longed to be, where she was once so easily happy. She became aware of the rhythmic motion of her breathing. So she concentrated on it for a while. In the silence she created, miracles took place.

Her wild beating heart quieted. The feeling of being lost disappeared. Her ears picked up on the songs of the park's birds and the wind tickling the leaves. Her personal world felt distant now. Her natural joy and curiosity for life flowed through her veins once again. She almost thought she was back home, rejoicing in the blessing of her garden.

And then, it hit her. She had just discovered how to always carry her sacred garden with her no matter where she found herself!

All Chelsea had to do was quiet her mind and body. Connect to her heart and breath. Mentally picture those glorious days. Then the comfort and peace from her garden would fill her heart and body once more. That day sitting under the willow tree, she made an important discovery. She could return to her country garden anytime, from anywhere she wanted. Oh happy day!

Chelsea jumped up and began to dance. The world looked wonderful and felt joyous again! The lightness returned to her body and spirit. She felt powerful, confident, and peaceful. She was ready to conquer the rest of her day.

Even after all those years of neglect, her precious garden still gave her gifts of wisdom. She understood how inside feelings could paint the colors of her outside world. She realized the importance of tending her inner garden. It would rebloom if given loving attention. Sometimes, the outside world is a little too noisy and a little bit too much. At those times, all she needs to do is connect to her glorious forever garden inside.

Do you...

... have a special place where you feel more joy, peace, and connection? This place can be real or imaginary. Describe the place. Be as detailed or vague as you would like. It's your place!

... feel differently when you are in your special space? Can you describe how you feel?

... carry these feelings from that space with you into the outside world?

... see many expressions of beauty in your day-to-day life just as it is? What are some of your favorites?

In *Chelsea's Forever Garden*, the creatures were happiest when they were themselves in their natural environment. Can you think of an instance where you were allowed to be your natural self? How did you feel? How about an instance when you allowed another to be their natural self?